CW00726457

THE ADVENTURES OF
Freddie Freckles

FR TIM'S TALES FOR CHRISTIAN CHILDREN

A Redemptorist Publication

Published by **Redemptorist Publications**
A Registered Charity limited by guarantee. Registered in England 3261721.

Text copyright © Timothy J. Buckley C.Ss.R., 2009
Illustrations copyright © Jane Morgan, 2009

First published October 2009
Reprinted March 2010

Layout: Rosemarie Pink
Cover design: Chris Nutbeen

ISBN 978-0-85231-370-1

All rights reserved. No part of this publication may be reproduced, stored in a retrieval system, or transmitted in any form or by any means, electronic, mechanical, photocopying, recording or otherwise, without prior permission in writing from Redemptorist Publications.

The moral right of Timothy Buckley to be identified as the author of this work has been asserted in accordance with the Copyright, Designs and Patents Act 1988.

A CIP catalogue record for this book is available from the British Library.

Printed by Lithgo Press Limited, Leicester LE8 6NU

Redemptorist
PUBLICATIONS
Alphonsus House Chawton Hampshire GU34 3HQ
Telephone 01420 88222 Fax 01420 88805
rp@rpbooks.co.uk   www.rpbooks.co.uk

Introduction

Enough people have encouraged me to write down the stories of Freddie Freckles to convince me that this book will be of service to those who, like myself, are fortunate enough to have opportunities, whether as priests, teachers, parents or catechists, to share the Gospel of Jesus with young children.

Jesus was the master storyteller and we all know how much children love a good story. Even in these days of complex multimedia presentations and computer games, a well-told story can still hold children's rapt attention and capture their imaginations.

On my first parish mission I witnessed at first hand the value of storytelling. Fr Michael Creech captivated his audience of primary school children by introducing Tommy and his sidekick, Freddie Freckles, as he explained the Gospel to them.

When I began to tell the same stories and add my own, Freddie Freckles took centre stage alongside his great friend Peter Pickles. In parishes and schools up and down the country, in which I have worked as a priest for almost forty years, generations of children have got to know these two characters and their friends.

Please note that each story, with its scriptural and liturgical connections, is offered as a separate entity. At the same time they are selected from a collection of stories I have used when giving a mission or working in a parish over a period of time, knowing that I would have a number of opportunities to meet the children. Some of the stories could be used in connection with Christmas, Lent, Easter and Pentecost, while others link with the sacraments of baptism, confirmation, the Eucharist and reconciliation.

Over the years I have found that it becomes easier to think up new stories to celebrate the different feasts or illustrate particular Gospel passages. My hope is that if you find this book helpful you will discover yourself doing the same. While it would be possible simply to read these stories to the children, there is no substitute for making them your own and adapting them for your own purposes. Better by far if you can memorise the story sufficiently to be able to tell it in your own words and even use different voices for the key characters... and particularly for Freddie himself. Adding your own personal touches, like catchphrases in current use, will bring the stories alive. Also, as a parent, teacher or catechist you may find occasions, at a later date, when you wish to recall the stories and reaffirm the morals behind them.

How to use this book

These stories have been used across key stages one and two, but Freddie is always a seven-year-old. This is the age when the majority of children still make their First Holy Communion and can begin to make more religious connections. My experience suggests that the younger ones can relate to someone just a couple of years older and the older children are happy to look back to the time when they were younger.

Good readers among the children may wish to read the stories for themselves.

Introductory notes to each story are offered for those who will be presenting the stories to groups of children; and they might begin by reminding the children: "Here is a story to help you remember what Jesus teaches us about..."

Contents

Freddie and the robot

Freddie and the robot

The lesson
The dignity of every person: each of us is unique, precious in the sight of God, made in the image of God.

Scripture references
The first creation story in Genesis:
> God created man in the image of himself,
> in the image of God he created him,
> male and female he created them. (Genesis 1:27)

Jesus reminds his disciples of their dignity:
> Why, every hair on your head has been counted...
> you are worth more than hundreds of sparrows. (Matthew 10:30. 31)

St Paul reminds us we are *children of God* (see Romans 8:16) and Peter reminds us that we are *a chosen race, a royal priesthood, a consecrated nation, a people set apart* (see 1 Peter 2:9).

When to tell this story
This story is ideal to introduce a group to Freddie Freckles.
It also works well as a one-off, teaching the most fundamental of all our beliefs: namely that God is our maker.

You will need time to tell this story well. It needs the build-up and the tension to be successful.

Notes
At the point in the story when the firefighter realises he can only save either the robot or Freddie you need to pause and hold the moment with the children. Then check with them: would they save the robot, or Freddie?

This is a story that rewards revisiting to discuss with the children the fact that they are all unique: the idea that they are all precious, that there will never be another Freddie or Peter or Harry or Katie or Erika or Petra or Mrs Kopek... you can go through the whole group; it will make a profound impression on them.

Freddie and the robot

My friend, Freddie Freckles, was crazy about robots. He first read about them in one of his magazines and after that he couldn't get enough of robots. He became particularly excited when he heard that a scientist had invented a robot that was so fantastic that it was going to be put on exhibition in one of the great museums in London.

His mum and dad had promised him they would take him to see the robot during the next holiday, but that was a few weeks away. Then something wonderful and exciting happened. Freddie went into school one morning and his teacher began the day with a big announcement. (He liked his teacher, Mrs Baxter, very much: she was strict but fair and she was always patient with the children when they didn't understand something.) She said: "I have been talking to the Head Teacher and he agrees with me that it would be a very good idea to have a class outing to London so that we can visit some of the museums." Freddie was so excited he couldn't wait to ask if they would be visiting the museum where the famous robot was. He put his hand up and asked the question and Mrs Baxter assured him he would be able to see the robot.

Freddie rushed home that evening and ran into the house, full of excitement and crying out to his mum: "Guess what, guess what, guess what!"

"Freddie, calm down, what is it?" she said.

"We're going on a school trip to see the robot."

"Well," said his mum, "you may go on the school trip if you are willing to put some of your pocket money towards the cost and if you stop moaning about what time you have to go to bed every night."

"I promise, Mum, I will be really good," he said. In fact for the next two weeks, leading up to the great trip, he was brilliant; even offering to do the washing-up after tea.

All the children in his class were going on the trip and getting more and more excited as the great day drew nearer. They had been divided into groups of six. Freddie and his friends, Peter and Harry, were with Katie and the twins, Erika and Petra. Mrs Kopek, the twins' mum, was the adult in charge of the group. Eventually the day arrived. They were all at school in good time and looking smart but casual, each with a rucksack and packed lunch and a few favourite toys for the journey; but "no mobiles", Mrs Baxter had said. They climbed up into the coach and found seats with their friends. Seat belts were buckled and off they went.

The friendly coach driver told the children little jokes as they went along. Then, when they got into the middle of London, he started pointing out lots of important places like the Houses of Parliament and Nelson's Column and Buckingham Palace. He even pointed out the famous shop Harrods, but told them the ice cream would be too expensive in there. No sooner had he said that than they were there in front of the science museum. It was huge and Freddie began to wonder how on earth he would find the robot.

They walked through huge doors into the entrance hall and stood together near a model of a spaceship.

Mrs Baxter said, "It is now half past ten. You have one hour, until half past eleven, to go wherever you want, but then I want you back here so that I can show you some important things before we have our packed lunches."

Freddie had been talking to everybody about the robot, so his group and some others had decided that the first thing they wanted to visit was the robot. A friendly man in uniform told them where to find it. "Boys and girls," he said, "it is right at the top of the museum. You will have to climb lots of stairs so I hope you are all fit."

"Yes we are," said the ones at the front and off they went, skipping up the stairs to the top of the museum. Poor Freddie... he was not very fit at this time... so by the time he got to the top of the museum he was out of breath and his group was right at the back of the crowd. They stuck together with Mrs Kopek.

He couldn't see anything, but one thing you need to know about Freddie is that he was a very patient little boy. So he waited and slowly but surely the children at the front tired of playing with the robot and Freddie began to get closer and closer, until after about twenty minutes Freddie's group were the only ones left.

Now Freddie was just so happy. He was pressing all the different buttons and the robot was moving this way and that and even answering the questions he had brought with him. For example, he had brought some of his maths homework and the robot was giving him the answers straightaway. After a few more minutes Harry and the girls and even his best friend Peter Pickles began to get bored and said, "Come on, Freddie, let's go and look at something else," but Freddie just said, "No, I'm staying. I've been waiting to see the robot for ages and I want to read all about it and try everything out."

However, after a few more minutes, Mrs Kopek firmly led them away and the group began walking down the stairs, chattering madly about clever scientists and amazing robots.

But Freddie Freckles had one last question for the robot; it wouldn't take a minute – he could catch them up. On a bend on the stairs, he let his friends go just ahead, turned tail, and raced back up to the robot. He spoke into its ear, "How far away is the nearest star?" and then, "What is 123 times 456?" Hey, this was SO good!

Freddie was jolted back into reality by the sound of his name: "Fredd...ie"! It was Mrs Kopek calling him. He looked round in the direction of her voice to see wisps of dust coming from the stairwell and the sound of coughing. It took only a second for Freddie to realise that the "dust" was smoke, and with it came the smell of burning.

"Run to the window, Freddie!" he heard Mrs Kopek splutter from the bend on the stairs. Freddie knew that he was on his own now, but in the distance he could hear people shouting. Suddenly a great siren went off and alarm bells began to ring. He ran to the window and saw lots of people on the pavement below, standing and pointing, looking up at the museum. Freddie's heart began to beat faster and faster. He turned and ran to the lift and pressed the button, but the sign came up "OUT OF ORDER". He ran back to the window. He could see people watching from behind a safety barrier, and there was Mrs Kopek and all the other children gathering at the assembly point. The first of the fire engines was heard racing down the road. Freddie pressed his little face against the window, his heart pounding fast and tears in his eyes. He waited and hoped.

Now you do need to know that the scientist we mentioned earlier, who had invented the robot, lived just around the corner from the museum. He had heard the commotion outside and the sound of the fire engines, so he rushed out of his house and saw the smoke coming from the museum. He dashed across the road and arrived just as the first of the fire engines was arriving. As the firefighters began to get their ladders and hoses organised he picked out the head firefighter and quickly shouted, "Please sir, at the very top of the museum is an amazing robot. It's been my life's work – it can do almost anything that we human beings can do. It cost millions of pounds to make… please, please, save it."

"I'll do my best, sir," said the head firefighter and as soon as the turntable ladder was in position, the head firefighter himself raced up. In no time he was at the window and he saw the robot sitting right in the centre of the museum. And then he saw Freddie.

Now the firefighter was very experienced. He had been fighting fires in London for thirty years and knew the fire was already so bad that it would not be long before the whole of the top floor was going to cave in, even though the sprinkler system would have switched on to slow down the progress of the fire. He realised therefore that he did not have time to save both the robot and Freddie.

I know who you would save and I know who I would save: yes –
Freddie.

Well, the head firefighter motioned to Freddie to stand back while
he broke the glass so that he could open the huge window. He picked
Freddie up and made his way down the ladder to safety. Just as they
reached the assembly point, there was a huge crash and the top floor did
collapse, as the firefighter knew it would, and the robot was destroyed.

The wonderful thing was that everyone, including the famous scientist,
wanted to congratulate the firefighter for saving Freddie.

Of course he had made the right choice in rescuing Freddie, because no
matter how many years it had taken to make the robot and no matter
how much money it had cost, you could always make another robot
exactly the same, but you could never make another Freddie.

Freddie and sports day

Freddie and sports day

The lesson

The friends of Jesus are to be like athletes in strict training. When we make sacrifices we can achieve great things.

Scripture references

St Paul tells the Corinthians:

> *All the runners at the stadium are trying to win, but only one of them gets the prize. You must run in the same way, meaning to win. All the fighters at the games go into strict training; they do this just to win a wreath that will wither away, but we do it for a wreath that will never wither.*
> (1 Corinthians 9:24-25)

Jesus told his disciples:

> *If anyone wants to be a follower of mine, let him renounce himself and take up his cross and follow me.* (Matthew 16:24)

Putting suffering into perspective for us, St Paul writes to the Romans:

> *I think that what we suffer in this life can never be compared to the glory, as yet unrevealed, which is waiting for us.* (Romans 8:18)

When to tell this story

The story is useful for the times when you are trying to encourage the children to make a special effort or to make some sacrifices. So it is ideal for the beginning of Lent or Advent.

Introduction

Have a chat with the children about the great athletes they know and get them to tell you about the training they have to do. Perhaps recall the most recent Olympic Games. From the 2008 Olympics, the UK can proudly remember many sportsmen and women, for example, Chris Hoy and Bradley Wiggins who won five gold medals between them for cycling, and Rebecca Adlington, who won two gold medals for swimming. These successful athletes have made many sacrifices to gain these results. They have trained for hours every day to achieve their goal.

Tell the children about Paul saying that the friends of Jesus have to be like runners in strict training if they want to be winners. The great news is that unlike the Olympic Games and all sporting events, Paul is saying that with Jesus everyone can be a winner and the prize will last for ever. Tease out with them what Paul means.

Paul is not worried about us winning races because he reminds us that next year we will probably have forgotten who won this year. Paul wants us all to train to be good and kind, loving and forgiving. He wants us to train to say "no" to ourselves and stop being selfish so that we can say "yes" to others when they need our help. We will find that this will not only make them happy but make us happy as well.

Freddie and sports day

Freddie was mad about all sports and he was a great trier, but he liked his iced buns too much and he was always one of the last in his class running race on sports day. However, this year he had been reading about how keen sportsmen and women practise for hours every week and how the great runners do regular training and keep to a strict exercise routine. A balanced diet was also important, with the right amount of energy and body-building foods and plenty of fruit and vegetables.

It was early in the summer term when he made his decision. The weather was good and outdoor games had begun. Although the school sports day was more than a month away, Freddie made a plan to begin training for the great day and surprise everyone.

First he had to get help from his neighbour, Rob, who was already in training for the town's "Charity Fun Run". Rob agreed to take Freddie on his early-morning runs before Freddie went to school and Rob went off to college.

Secondly, he would need help from his mum: "Please, Mum, tomorrow morning I want to get up half an hour early and go for a run." His mum was very impressed and said, "Certainly, Freddie, I'll call you, but what's this all about?" Then he told her about his ambition to do better on sports day: how he was going to swap iced buns and chocolate for apples and oranges. He told his mum that she could tell his dad and his sister, Suzie, that he was going to train with Rob next door, but no one else must know… it was to be a secret. He was determined to surprise everyone when the great day came.

Freddie usually got up at seven-thirty, so at seven o'clock the next morning, according to his instructions, his mum tapped gently at the door of his bedroom. He woke up and saw the time on his bedside clock and wondered what was happening. Then he remembered his decision and thought better of it. "Please go away, Mum," he shouted. "Tell Rob I've changed my mind." His mum gently opened the door and went over to Freddie, tickling him under the chin and saying, "Go on, Freddie, have a go… you'll feel great when you come back in for breakfast."

"No, honestly," he said, "I've changed my mind." But his mum gently encouraged him and eventually a rather grumpy Freddie got out of bed and put on his tracksuit. He did remember to say a little prayer and offer the day to God, and then he went out to find Rob waiting for him.

Freddie got started but very quickly he was panting and he got a pain in his side, so he stopped and walked the rest of the way. When he came back about ten minutes later he flopped down at the breakfast table and said, "I'm never ever going to do that again." His mum smiled and said, "But, Freddie, it will get easier each day."

"That's what Rob said, but no," he said, "never again." Next morning, his mum knocked at the door again and this time Freddie got cross and shouted, "Mum, I told you no!" It took his mum a long time to coax him, but she managed and eventually he got up in a very bad mood. This time Rob suggested that he run for a short time then walk for a short time and so on until he had covered the distance. He didn't get the pain, so he was back in the house after eight minutes.

His mum didn't say anything but gave him a breakfast of cereal, banana and a boiled egg with a thick slice of buttered brown bread. She noticed that he didn't say anything about not doing it again. By the end of the first week, when his mum called him he was crying out, "OK, Mum, I don't want to, but I'll get up," and he was finding that he could run a little further each day.

And so the regular training went on. Now and then Freddie felt like saying, "I think I'll leave the training for tomorrow," but his mum was able to encourage him to keep on going.

After three weeks Freddie was beginning to look very fit. Suzie, who was watching Freddie's progress with great interest, was beginning to get very excited. She was tempted to tell her friends what was happening, but she was very good and didn't say a word to anyone. As sports day approached, Freddie could run 400 metres in just one minute thirty and he knew he was going to do well, but he could not be sure of beating Peter and Tom, who were the two really good runners in his class.

When the great day arrived, the weather was beautiful: sunny and warm, and everyone was very excited. The school field had been prepared for all the events. There was bunting everywhere and chairs for the parents and guests. The afternoon began with a little speech from the Head Teacher, who welcomed everyone and reminded the children that the important things were taking part and doing your best.

The time came for Freddie's race over 400 metres, which was twice round the school field. Mrs Baxter, his teacher, lined them up and then the Head Teacher said: "On your marks, get set, GO!"

They set off and, as expected, Peter and Tom were soon in the lead. However, to everyone's surprise, there was Freddie Freckles tucked in behind them in third place. Rob had told him not to go for the line too soon. The three boys began to build a lead over all the other children. As they came round the field for the second time Freddie couldn't believe how good he was feeling. His stomach was tucked in, his chest was out, his hair was flowing back in the wind and his little legs were pounding away, but he didn't feel tired. He was breathing really well.

At the same time he noticed that both Peter and Tom were beginning to lose their rhythm. At this point they looked round to see Freddie right on their heels. Freddie registered their shocked expressions and then it happened. As he came round the last bend he went racing past them. Into the final straight he was already five metres ahead of them, and now he could see the winning tape ahead. There was nothing Peter or Tom could do. Freddie won the race by ten metres!

As he passed the line he went down on his knees in triumph; he knew he had done it; all his training had paid off. Everyone was so excited: his mum, his dad, Suzie, his teacher and the others in his class. Even

Peter and Tom were generous in their disappointment and came over to Freddie to congratulate him on his wonderful effort. It was only then that they learnt about Freddie's training over the previous weeks. Freddie had a lot to thank Rob for, *and* his family for their great support.

Freddie had won the prize on sports day.

Freddie asks the way

Freddie asks the way

The lesson
Understanding the meaning of faith; we put our faith in people. The Christian believes in the person of Jesus, not in a set of beliefs or a way of life. Our beliefs and our way of life follow from putting our faith and trust in Jesus.

Scripture references
When Jesus tells the disciples that they know the way to the place he is going to, Thomas asks how they can know the way when they don't know where he is going. Jesus says to Thomas:

I am the Way, the Truth and the Life. (John 14:6)

Later, when Thomas doubts whether Jesus has risen from the dead, Jesus will say to him:

Doubt no longer but believe. (John 20:27)

When to tell this story
In today's world children have to be taught from an early age that there are dangers and that not everyone can be trusted. Jesus taught his disciples to be careful not to follow people who would mislead them (the false prophets): *You will be able to tell them by their fruits* (Matthew 7:16). This story is designed to help children understand what it means to say, "I believe."

Introduction
It will be useful to chat with the children about Jesus' conversations with Thomas and tease out with them where they think Jesus was actually going. When you have established that it is heaven, you might then ask them what they think Jesus means by saying that he is "the Way". He is telling us that the straight path to heaven is to live good lives: to be kind and thoughtful and forgiving. We can put our faith in him because we know we can trust him from the way he loved people, and because of all the good things he did for them. If you are telling this story during the Easter season you may wish to focus on the resurrection as the means whereby Jesus gets to heaven, and eventually we get there too.

Freddie asks the way

Freddie was a very lucky boy. Every year his mum and dad saved up enough to take him and his sister Suzie on holiday to the seaside. Last year they had such a great holiday that they had decided to go back to the same place. As the holiday got nearer, Freddie got more and more excited. He loved the beach, swimming, body-surfing, fishing, and catching crabs in the rock pools.

He had packed his rucksack days before they were due to leave and he kept checking that he had remembered everything. Certainly he had not forgotten a good spade for digging, his kite and his body-board. He even had a wetsuit this year.

When the day arrived he woke up early and was up, washed and dressed long before the rest of the family. Mum was busy locking windows and doing a last clean and putting the rubbish out. Dad was filling every space in the boot of the car and around Freddie's and Suzie's seats until all the luggage was in.

Freddie was sent next door with the spare key for Rob's parents, who had promised to keep an eye on the house for them. Rob had helped Freddie with training for sports day a few weeks before. They could see how excited Freddie was. "Are you looking forward to your holiday, Freddie?" they said. "Oh yes," he said, "I can't wait to see the sea again and go down to play on the beach. The other exciting thing is that my Aunty Maggie is going to join us on holiday and I will be able to show her all my favourite places."

Rob's parents gave Freddie some extra pocket money to share with Suzie. He said, "Thank you," with a big smile and raced back home to give Suzie her share. His mum and dad said that they couldn't wish for kinder neighbours.

Aunty Maggie would be coming after work by train from London. Freddie and his family would have time to settle into their holiday cottage before collecting her from the station.

The car journey seemed to go on for ever, but with his travel bag close at hand, packed with pens, puzzle books and some favourite treasures, he and Suzie kept each other happy.

A break for their packed lunch with an extra treat or two and already they were in holiday mood. They made their way to the coast, speeding past fields of cattle and sheep and fields of corn turning yellow in the summer sun. The familiar London scenery was soon out of their minds.

The holiday cottage was just as Freddie had remembered, painted white with a blue door and blue windowframes. Dad drove off to collect Aunty Maggie while Freddie and Suzie unpacked and sorted out the rooms. Delicious smells were coming from the kitchen as mum got the dinner on.

Freddie checked the garden out: a swing and climbing frame down one end; a wooden table with benches on the patio and best of all, in the distance, the blue, blue sea. He couldn't wait to… but there was Aunty Maggie bursting through the house. Freddie knew she couldn't wait either, to run down to the sandy beach and touch the sea.

"Mum, I just *have* to take Aunty Maggie to have a quick look at the sea – please, Mum?"

"Just a quick look now, Freddie," chorused his mum, dad and sister.

Freddie was bursting with excitement as he pulled Aunty Maggie along, saying, "I'm going to show you the best sandy beach ever."

They hurried along the pavement in the direction of the sea, through the park bright with flowers, along by the putting green. "I'll be back there later," Freddie thought. He remembered that he would now have to go through the town before getting down to the beach, and he saw the little Town Hall and next to it the old Tudor-style building that was the Tourist Office. But then he stopped still because he just couldn't remember which way to turn. Everything looked just like any other town: a Post Office, W.H. Smith, Marks and Spencer, and the rest of the shops.

"Are you lost, Freddie?" asked Aunty Maggie. She was just about to suggest going back to the Tourist Office when Freddie was off like a hare. He had spotted a policeman across the shopping precinct and by the time Aunty Maggie caught up with him the policeman was already pointing him in the right direction. Freddie had remembered that the police in this seaside town always seemed to be smiling and friendly and helpful, and he shook the policeman's hand, saying, "Thank you very much." In no time he had followed the directions perfectly and he and Aunty Maggie had arrived at the best sandy beach ever. They stood for a few moments and thought of all the fun they were going to have during the holiday, and then they both agreed to go straight back to the cottage, knowing that the meal would be ready when they returned.

Aunty Maggie didn't miss an opportunity. "What a friendly policeman he was, Freddie." "Yes," said Freddie, "I remembered from last year how helpful the policeman was when Dad couldn't remember how to get somewhere."

"You know," said Aunty Maggie, "it reminds me of when I was your age and we were always told to ask a policeman the way. Our teacher told us that you should only ever ask the way of someone you can trust and she then told us that is why we should listen so carefully to all the directions Jesus gives us when he is telling us how to live our lives and how to get to heaven."

"That's a good point," said Freddie, "I'll remember that." And just as they finished this conversation they were back at the cottage and ready for dinner.

Freddie learns to swim

Freddie learns to swim

The lesson
It is always good to help children to learn the value of silence and relaxing. This story is designed to help them think about prayer, not just as something we have to do, but as something which helps us to relax in the presence of God.

Scripture references
Matthew 6:5-13: Jesus teaches us how to pray and not to babble.

Romans 8:26-27: Paul reminds us that the Holy Spirit is already praying within us.

When to tell this story
This story could be used at any time, but in particular as an introduction to the Holy Spirit and Pentecost. Encourage the children to think about the value of a balanced life. The way we behave, the way we think and the way we pray are all important.

Introduction
Check how many of the children can swim and how they learnt to swim. See if any are still fearful of the water. You might also wish to explore with them the idea that sometimes the harder we try to do certain things, the more difficult they seem to become. This may ring true for some children who find things like sport difficult, but it may also be true for others in different areas of life including certain school lessons, not to mention trying to pray.

The end of this story could be a good time to invite the children to be silent and spend a few quiet moments imagining themselves lying back in God's arms. You could end the session by saying "Amen".

Freddie learns to swim

Freddie was really troubled about one thing in particular and that was that he couldn't swim. Some of his friends were really good swimmers. For example, Peter Pickles had already swum ten lengths of the swimming baths to help raise money for the local children's hospice, and other friends, both boys and girls, were always off to the swimming pool and loved swimming at the sea when they were on holiday.

Freddie had become frightened of the water when he was very young because one day a big wave had swept him off his feet when he was paddling in the sea. By the time he had struggled to his feet and got his head out of the water he had swallowed a lot of salty seawater. His mum and dad tried to reassure him that he was all right and that they were there, but although he loved splashing about in the water he watched the waves very carefully after that. Every summer he tried to learn to swim, but he never managed to trust the water enough to let himself go.

Then one summer he decided that this was going to be the year he would learn to swim. He had overheard a conversation his sister Suzie was having with her friend. She was telling Suzie that she had learnt to swim by learning to float in shallow seawater.

"Because of all the salt in the seawater, it holds you up much more easily than the water in a swimming pool," she was saying, and he remembered she used the word "buoyant". That was it... Freddie had decided he was going to find a quiet place at the seaside that summer and learn to float.

On the first day of his summer holiday, the whole family as usual went off to the beach with their cool box full of food and drink, and all the suntan lotion, beach mats, chairs, spades and buckets that helped them enjoy themselves for the whole day. Freddie couldn't wait to try his experiment in the water. He quickly changed into his swimming trunks and ran down to the water's edge. It was cold at first, but quickly he got used to it and the sea was lovely and calm. He was sure this was the day he would learn to float. He hadn't said anything to his mum and dad or Suzie, and they just thought he was enjoying his usual splash around.

Freddie shouted to them that he was going down by the rocks to look for some crabs and they had said, "OK, but be careful." Among the rocks there was a shallow pool of water that the sea had left as the tide had gone out and Freddie decided this was the place to learn to float. Carefully he rolled over onto his back, threw his head back and stretched his arms out. Then he allowed his legs to rise off the sand until he felt the water holding him up. He could hardly believe it: he had done it at the first attempt; and then he began to kick his legs up and down in excitement.

Soon he came out of his little pool and wandered back along the water's edge to the main beach, where he could see lots of people swimming and some just still, floating on the water. Freddie decided to do the same on the open sea and it worked. He was so excited and, realising that the water really would take his weight, he now turned over onto his front and began to push out and swim. In less than a quarter of an hour it had all happened.

"Is that Freddie swimming?" his mum said to his dad a few minutes later.

"I do believe it is," said his dad, who waded in slowly, taking care not to worry him.

Freddie and his dad practised their swimming together. It seemed amazingly easy.

It was a fantastic day for Freddie because that evening his parents gave him a special treat back at their holiday cottage. There was a flat-looking parcel lying on the wooden table. Freddie unwrapped it and inside there was a rubber dinghy all creased and tightly folded. Dad pumped it into life with a foot pump and Suzie and Freddie tried it out for size. Dad attached a strong length of rope to the loop in the bow, and there it was ready for playing with in the sea the next day. Freddie had no fear now of jumping in under the waves, he knew that he had to hold his breath and then come up to the surface like a buoyant buoy!

Before he went to bed that evening, his dad was ready as usual to tell him a story and say his night prayers with him. The story that night was about his dad.

"Do you know, Freddie," he said, "I learnt to swim in exactly the same way as you did. And afterwards I often thought about the times I had thrashed about in the water trying to stay afloat. In fact it made me think that sometimes I do something similar when I am trying to pray.

It is not always easy and often I struggle to think about holy things and about God. If I am finding it very difficult, then I stop trying, and I think of myself lying on top of the sea. You know, prayer really is like that. When I stop struggling I just lie back and rest in the arms of God. That's as good a way as any to pray. Jesus tells us not to babble away like people who do not have any real faith in him. Also, St Paul tells us that God's Spirit is already inside us doing the praying for us.

"So shall we just do that tonight? Lie back in God's arms and say a big 'thank you'."

Freddie lay back in his bed and, as he became sleepy, his dad just said, "Amen. God bless you, Freddie, and have lots of good dreams."

Freddie and the
dangerous waters

Freddie and the dangerous waters

The lesson
Even when we are unhappy or frightened, Jesus is always there, wanting to look after us.

Scripture reference
Without warning a storm broke over the lake, so violent that the waves were breaking right over the boat. But Jesus was asleep. So the disciples went to him and woke him saying, "Save us, Lord, we are going down!" And he said to them, "Why are you so frightened, you men of little faith?" And with that he stood up and rebuked the winds and the sea; and all was calm again. (Matthew 8:24-26)

When to tell this story
Young children have their worries and it is good for them to feel the security of their parents and teachers, their friends and relatives, and to know that their reassurance is built on the firm belief that Jesus is always with us.

Introduction
Discuss with the children the things which make them frightened and anxious and what they do in those situations.

Freddie and the dangerous waters

Now Freddie really loved his holidays at the seaside. One year his mum and dad promised that as he had learnt to swim, they would take him out in a boat. They picked a beautiful sunny day when the forecast promised fine weather all day, and went down to the river to hire a boat. His dad said that it would be safer to row up and down the river than to go on the open sea. They got into the boat and his dad, who was very strong and a good rower, eased the boat out onto the water and began to row upstream. He rowed very smoothly and they had gone a long way when Freddie's mum suggested they stop for lunch. His dad gently steered the boat towards the bank, where they were able to moor it.

His mum had made a brilliant packed lunch with lots of extra treats and they ate until they were full. They lay back in the sun and listened to the sound of water lapping against the bottom of the boat. Apart from the seagulls wheeling overhead and the insects in the grassy bank they were completely alone. After a while they clambered aboard and began the journey back to the boat-hire station where they had begun their trip earlier in the day. Freddie was simply loving the experience. The water was beautifully clear and he could see the fish swimming around. As they were rowing, Freddie's dad reminded him and Suzie of how often Jesus had got into a boat with his disciples. It was an important means of transport in Jesus' day and some of his disciples were fishermen and very experienced boatmen.

Then, suddenly and unexpectedly, the wind got up and huge dark clouds began to gather overhead. "This wasn't part of the forecast," said Freddie's dad. The wind stirred up the water into choppy waves which bumped against the sides of the boat. Dad was having to work really hard to keep the boat steady as he rowed against the wind. Then the rain began, the wind driving it into the frightened group in the boat. All the time Freddie's dad used his loud voice telling them not to worry, that he would get them back safely. There was a flash of lightning and a huge clap of thunder and the rain began to fall in torrents, but *still* Freddie's dad told them that all would be well. In spite of their cagoules and life jackets it was still very scary.

The waves were forcing the boat up in the air and down again, but Freddie's dad was true to his word. He rowed like an expert and eventually the boathouse appeared. Then as they came to the riverbank, as quickly as it had started, the rain stopped and the sun came out. They tied up the boat and greeted the boatman, who said, "Well done, that was a sudden and very violent storm." Looking at Freddie's dad, he said, "You must be a strong rower to have kept going in that weather."

"I learnt to row as a schoolboy," Freddie's dad said, "and remembered all the tricks of the trade." Then he added, "But I said a little prayer as well, reminding Jesus that he had calmed the storm for the disciples when they were caught in a storm at sea."

Freddie's dad decided that a good strong cup of tea was in order and soon they were to be found drying off in a teashop, having tea and chunks of flapjack, all the while chatting about their exciting but somewhat frightening experience.

Freddie stargazes

Freddie stargazes

The lesson
Children have a natural sense of wonder. This story is designed to explore the wonder of the world about us and indeed of the whole universe, and link it with the biblical sense of standing in awe before the presence of God.

Scripture references
Psalm 148 is a psalm that helps us stand in awe before creation.

Matthew 2:1-11 tells the story of the visit of the wise men.

When to tell this story
Because of the Epiphany connection, this story could be added to the Christmas list, but it could also be used at other times, placing the emphasis on the wonders of creation.

Introduction
Discuss with the children the meaning of the word "wonderful". What makes them full of wonder? What makes them think: "That's amazing"?

Freddie stargazes

Because Freddie lived near London with all the traffic and the street lights he had never really seen the sky dark at night; there was always the glow of the city lighting up the sky. So one day during their holidays away in the country, his mum and dad told him that as a special treat he could stay up until after dark and see the stars. That year they were staying in a little village near the seaside and the only lights in the village came from the windows of the cottages and the village pub. If you were out at night it was necessary to take a torch to find your way in the darkness of the night.

That year Peter Pickles had come on holiday with Freddie, while Freddie's sister Suzie had joined the Pickles family on their holiday.

Staying up late to see the stars in the night sky was going to be really exciting. It had been a beautiful day and the sun had been shining brilliantly. His mum and dad had planned everything very carefully.

They knew that it would be the night of the full moon and the forecast was for a perfectly clear night to follow the sunny day. The sun was low in the sky as they left their holiday cottage.

"Right, boys, let's watch the sunset and see if we can identify some famous planets and stars." Freddie's dad did not know much about the stars, but he had been brought up in the country and found looking up at the stars at night quite breathtaking. His mum had studied astronomy as part of her course at university, so she was more of an expert. However, tonight both his mum and dad just wanted Freddie to have one of those breathtaking experiences.

Freddie could never remember seeing a sunset quite like this one. As the sun got lower and lower in the sky it turned into an amazing red ball and it was possible to look at it in a way you could never do when it was shining brightly in the middle of the day. He thought it was absolutely beautiful and then he noticed that, even before the sun disappeared, the moon could be seen quite clearly.

During the next forty minutes he and Peter whispered quietly to each other as the sun gradually disappeared and the moon took over lighting up the sky. It was breathtakingly beautiful. They were reminded that the light from the moon was actually coming from the sun, which also shines upon the moon, because the moon is a satellite of the earth: in other words, just as the moon goes round the earth, so the earth goes round the sun. And then they began to look for the other great stars of our system, which is called the solar system, because it revolves around the sun: the word solar means "of the sun". These great stars are called planets and one or two, like Mars and Venus, are usually easy to spot.

Freddie's mum and dad told the boys to stand still and see if they could count all the stars in the sky. They soon realised that they were impossible to count: there were thousands and thousands of tiny lights twinkling in the sky. All this is part of the galaxy we call the "Milky Way" and Freddie's mum explained that the solar system was only a small part of this great galaxy. Then she told them that there are millions of other galaxies in outer space.

Freddie and Peter listened, but just couldn't take in the size and the numbers: it seemed quite extraordinary, but Freddie sensed that God must be very great indeed to have created all this; and here were he and Peter, just tiny little specks in this huge universe.

Somehow Freddie's dad realised what he was thinking: it was what he himself had thought when he was a little boy looking up into the sky. So he said to Freddie and Peter, "It's just amazing, isn't it? And think that in the midst of all this, God loved us so much that he sent Jesus to us to help us live good lives and to make sure that we remain his friends."

"Are there other people out there on the planets and in the other galaxies?" asked Peter and Freddie together.

"No one knows," said dad, "but if there are, then we can be sure that God will love them and look after them too."

Then his dad reminded the boys of the story of the wise men coming from the east and how they used one of the stars to guide them to find Jesus.

"How did they know which star to follow?" said Freddie.

"No one really knows that either," said his dad, "but we do know that they were clever men and of course they were attentive to God in their prayers. So God guided them to the place they needed to be. That, Freddie and Peter, is why it is so important that we say our prayers and try to notice the wonder of God all around us. Some people get so selfish and so concerned about trying to make themselves happy that they forget about everyone else and don't notice all the beautiful things God has made to make them happy. Unlike the wise men who brought their precious gifts to the baby Jesus, such people think only about receiving gifts, and never about giving them. There is no doubt that the more generous we are and the more filled with wonder we are, the happier we will be. So let's say a big 'thank you' to God for this beautiful night sky."

So with their torches shining beams of light on their path ahead, Peter and Freddie made their way back to their cottage. It had truly been an awesome experience gazing at the night sky.

Freddie and the teddy bear

Freddie and the teddy bear

The lesson

When we are generous and kind, we receive far more than we give away. We give presents to show that we love one another; and God has given us the greatest gift of all, Jesus his Son. This is why we celebrate Christmas, the birth of Jesus, as the great time for giving presents.

Scripture references

Jesus teaches us:

> *Give, and there will be gifts for you: a full measure, pressed down, shaken together, and running over, will be poured into your lap.* (Luke 6:38)

Jesus explains to Nicodemus:

> *God loved the world so much that he gave his only Son, so that everyone who believes in him… may have eternal life.* (John 3:16)

When to tell this story

This story is obviously linked with Christmas, but it can be used all through the year. Children love to think about Christmas and its meaning. The story will help them to think about being generous because God has been generous to us and always wants what is best for us.

Freddie and the teddy bear

If there was one thing Freddie just didn't like doing, it was going shopping. His sister, Suzie, loved it. She never got bored with looking at new clothes and shoes. However, it was nearly Christmas and his mum needed his help to carry all the bags of presents and extra food. Freddie trailed along, getting more and more tired and more and more fed up.

"Oh when will we be finished?" he kept asking, and his mum would say, "Just a couple more presents, one for Aunty Maggie and one for Uncle Chris," and no sooner had they been bought than she would remember someone else.

Then, wonder of wonders, Freddie noticed a big sign which read: FATHER CHRISTMAS → THIS WAY.

"Look, Mum," said Freddie, "may I go and visit Father Christmas please?"

"You have been very good and helpful Freddie, just be patient for a little while longer and yes, you may."

Eventually they returned to the Father Christmas sign and Freddie went to go in. It was so late in the day that it was almost closing time and Father Christmas was just about to pack up and go home, but he saw Freddie approaching and stayed in his grotto.

"Hello, young man," said Father Christmas. "What's your name?"

"My name is Freddie Freckles," said Freddie, who then carried on, "I know you are only a pretend Father Christmas because the real Father Christmas is St Nicholas, who was very kind and generous and, like Jesus, he wanted all the children to be looked after and happy. He wants children to receive nice presents at Christmas but also to *give* nice presents at Christmas."

"My word, you are a knowledgeable little boy," said Father Christmas. "And because you are such a friendly little chap, here is a little early Christmas present for you."

"Thank you," said Freddie. "Whatever it is, I am grateful".

They wished each other "Happy Christmas" and Freddie went skipping back to his mum and sister. His mum said he could open the present; and it was a brown furry teddy bear. Secretly Freddie was really pleased but he said, "Oh, I'm getting too old for teddy bears; I was hoping he would give me a football or something useful."

Just after he had finished saying this, they reached the front door of the shop. There were loads of people outside and it was very difficult to get through the crowd. Then Freddie realised something was wrong. It was raining and he could hear a little girl crying. He pushed his way through the crowd to see what was happening and there was this little girl, she was only about five, and straightaway he could see what had happened. She must have tripped over as she came out of the shop and there lying next to her in a big dirty pool of water was a teddy bear, exactly the same as the one Father Christmas had given to him. It was completely ruined.

"Oh dear," said Freddie, "is that your teddy?" She was crying so much you could hardly hear her mutter, "yes".

"Here you are; this is for you," said Freddie as he gave her his teddy. She could hardly believe what was happening; and then as she took the teddy she stopped crying and began to say, "Thank you, thank you, thank you," her voice growing stronger all the time. She even went to give Freddie a big hug, but he said, "It's OK: have a good Christmas," and he pushed through the crowd back to his mum.

At that moment all the people standing around began to cheer and clap and say to one another, "What a kind little boy; that is the real Christmas spirit." His mum and sister felt tremendously proud of him.

The amazing thing was that as they travelled home Freddie, even though he would really have loved to have kept his teddy bear, began to feel better and better, happier and happier. And that is what happens when we behave unselfishly and make other people happy. We become happy too.

Freddie and the parish crib

Freddie and the parish crib

The lesson
This story has to do with building a sense of community around the
Christmas story and has its origins in a custom I encountered once in a
particular parish.

Scripture reference
Luke gives us the Christmas story in more detail than any of the other
Gospels. See Luke 1:26-56; 2:1-20.

When to tell this story
In the season of Advent or just before, especially if there is the possibility
that your parish might wish to introduce the custom.

Introduction
Take time to discuss with the children the value and significance of
ornaments and statues at home and in school.

Note
There are some reasonably priced cribs around. The one used in the
parish where this custom began was made out of plastic and was almost
impossible to damage, but still the figures were beautifully crafted.

Freddie and the parish crib

Freddie always loved Christmas time and this year it was going to be very special because he was in the First Communion class. In his parish they had a wonderful custom which meant that during the four weeks leading up to Christmas, the time we call Advent, which means "Coming", each of the families with children in the First Communion class had a special crib in their home for just one night. Peter Pickles' family had had the crib the night before and they were all coming to Freddie's house at six o'clock.

There was great excitement getting everything ready. Freddie had his tea as soon as he came home from school and then went straight to the corner of the room where the crib was going to be placed. His dad had made a wonderful cave out of cardboard and brown paper and Freddie had helped to put the paint on the night before. His dad had explained to Freddie that the stable where Jesus was born might well have been a cave, a rough place next to the house, but somewhere to keep the animals warm and dry at night. When they had finished building the cave they had put straw on the floor to make it look like a real stable. His dad and Suzie, his sister, arrived home as promised in time for the arrival of the crib.

Freddie couldn't wait and was on the doorstep at five to six when he saw the Pickles family come round the corner. Freddie had invited lots of his friends round as well and he noticed his little friend Francisco was among a group following Mr and Mrs Pickles and Peter and their other children. Freddie loved the Italian name for Francis (Francisco) and he knew that it was the great St Francis of Assisi who, eight hundred years ago, had built the first crib so that the people would see what Christmas must really have been like.

Peter Pickles was carrying the lantern which was part of the crib as well as lighting up the way for everyone. As they got closer he could hear them singing a beautiful carol and realised that it was being led by Francisco and his family. It was Italy's favourite carol, "Tu scendi dalle stelle", "From starry skies descending", just as we have our favourite ones like "Silent Night" and "Away in a Manger."

Everyone was welcomed by Mr and Mrs Freckles, Freddie and his sister Suzie. The crib figures had all been carefully wrapped up in a big box and they were put down in front of Freddie's prepared stable in the corner of the room. Then his mum got drinks for all the adults and the children had fruit juice. There were lots of mince pies and some other nice food to nibble and for the next half an hour everyone chatted and talked about their plans for Christmas.

When they had finished their drinks and food, Peter and his mum and dad handed over a beautifully bound book with all the details about how to assemble the crib, and readings from the Gospel story of Christmas. It also had a page for each family to write down what it had been like for them to have the crib in their house and the Pickles family had filled the page with the thoughts of their children and some lovely drawings as well.

Now the Pickles family left, and wished everyone a very happy evening, and it was time for Freddie and his other friends to unpack the crib and put it all together. Every statue had a number and Mr Freckles laid everything out in order. Mrs Freckles opened the book at the readings and then they began, first taking Joseph and Mary out of their wrappings and placing them in the crib.

Different children were chosen to read the short passages explaining who everyone was and what part they had to play in the story. There were angels and shepherds, the wise men and their gifts, a wonderful star that fitted onto the top of the cave, little lambs and an ox and an ass. When all the little statues were placed, Mr Freckles said, "Someone very important is missing."

"It's Jesus," all the children said in chorus. And sure enough the last package to be unpacked was Jesus lying in a manger, which formed his little bed. Very carefully Jesus was placed in the centre of the crib and all the children knelt down and said the prayer that was in the book:

Dear Jesus, we thank you for coming into our world to bless all children and help us to live good and happy lives. Help us to look after one another and especially those children who are not as lucky as we are, by always being generous and kind. Bless our families and friends. Watch over us and protect us from all harm. May your holy angels be here to keep us in peace and may your blessing be always upon us. Amen.

Then they sang "Away in a Manger".

The time had passed amazingly quickly, but they realised it had taken them over an hour to put the crib together.

The children's questions had been answered and everyone was satisfied that all the statues were in the right place. After his friends had gone home and right up to bedtime Freddie kept going back and checking the crib, watching the lantern burn gently beside it and thinking what an amazingly beautiful story it was.

He was sad to think that he was going to have to give the crib away the following day, but his mum and dad had thought of everything and his dad had made some beautiful crib figures in his workshop, which they would put in the crib on Christmas Eve. They would have their own crib in the corner of the room all through the Christmas season until after the wise men had visited on the feast of the Epiphany on 6th January.

Freddie and his sister, Suzie, wrote some beautiful thoughts in the book about having the crib in their house. Can you think what sort of things Freddie and his sister might have written?

Freddie and his sick grandma

Freddie and his sick grandma

The lesson
This is a story to illustrate the importance of Jesus' teaching that we are to visit and care for people who are sick. Again it illustrates that when we make others happy we are made happy, but first we have to overcome our selfishness. It is also an opportunity to introduce the children to the idea that whatever we do for each other, we do for Jesus.

Scripture references
I was hungry and you gave me food; I was thirsty and you gave me drink… sick and you visited me… (Matthew 25:35. 36)

And wherever he [Jesus] went, to village, or town, or farm, they laid down the sick in the open spaces, begging him to let them touch even the fringe of his cloak. (Mark 6:56)

Because Freddie doesn't always understand why he behaves in the way he does, you might also want to make a reference to the fact that often people (adults as well!) don't understand their behaviour. Even St Paul says he doesn't understand his own behaviour: *I cannot understand my own behaviour. I fail to carry out the things I want to do, and I find myself doing the very things I hate* (Romans 7:15).

When to tell this story
The heart of Jesus' message is LOVE. We show our love by the way we look after each other. This story is designed to take us to the heart of the Gospel and how it is to be lived. It could be used at any time.

Introduction
Preparing the children for this story: do they remember times when they stamped their feet and said "no"?

Talk about how often Jesus visited sick people and made them better. Remind them of the passage in Matthew's Gospel quoted above, where Jesus assures us that whatever kindness we do to others we do to him. The meaning of this could be explored by reminding the children that at baptism they all became children of God.

Freddie and his sick grandma

It was Saturday morning and Freddie was up early because he had planned to go out and play football with Peter, Tom and a few of his other friends. Peter's dad had said that he would take them up to the park if they all went round to Peter's house.

When he came downstairs, dressed in his tracksuit and ready for football, his mum was already getting the breakfast, and she told him that last night, after he had gone to bed, Grandma had phoned to say she wasn't feeling very well. Grandma lived just round the corner so his mum had gone round to see her and make her comfortable for the night.

"After breakfast, Freddie," his mum said, "would you just pop round and see Grandma and check if she needs anything before I go out shopping? I'll give you the key, but knock first and then as you go in call up to Grandma to let her know it is you."

Freddie was sorry that Grandma wasn't well but he wanted to go out and play football, so, to the surprise of his mum, he just blurted out: "I can't go; I'm going to play football."

"Freddie, you'll do as you're told," his mum said.

"I won't," he said, and stamped his foot and ran out of the kitchen and up to his bedroom crying. Freddie was all confused. He loved his grandma but he had set his heart on playing football and he was afraid that if he didn't arrive at Peter's in time they would go to the park without him. Even so, he couldn't understand why he had behaved so badly.

He was still in a bad mood when he crept downstairs. He picked up the key from the table, passed his mum and muttered, "I'm going to see Grandma."

When he got to Grandma's house he slipped in and shouted up the stairs to let her know it was him. As he went into the room her face lit up and she said, "Oh Freddie, how kind of you to come and see me. You have made me feel better already, just by coming; and you must have got lots of things you want to do today." Freddie was all confused and didn't dare tell Grandma what had just happened at home.

He said, "That's all right: Mum said you hadn't been feeling very well. Is there anything I can do?"

"Well Freddie," she said, "you see the tea-maker on the cupboard? Would you please switch it on? I would love a cup of tea."

"OK," said Freddie, and in no time the tea was made and Freddie had poured Grandma a cup and sat down by her side. She chatted away about the old times when she had been a little girl and all the things they used to get up to on Saturday mornings, and she began to show Freddie some old photographs of her when she was growing up. He became more and more fascinated and forgot all about the football as they sat there chatting for over an hour. In fact Freddie's mum had crept round and let herself into the house to see what was going on, but when she heard them chatting away, she just smiled to herself and crept out again.

Eventually Grandma sat up and stretched her arms and said, "Do you know, Freddie, I feel much better. In fact I am going to get up and get some fresh air as it is such a nice day. Thank Mum for coming round last night and tell her that your visit this morning completed my recovery. Now go and enjoy yourself."

Freddie ran back to the house and told his mum and dad the news. Nothing else was said about Freddie's behaviour at breakfast. He knew that he was forgiven and his mum and dad knew that Freddie had learnt an important lesson.

Then his dad said, "Come on, Freddie, into the car. Peter's dad phoned and told me where he was taking them to play football. I'll take you round."

Freddie and the power cut

Freddie and the power cut

The lesson
Jesus speaks of himself as the light of the world and then tells us that **we** are to be the light of the world. We do this by being shining examples to other people of how to live good and happy lives.

Scripture references
Jesus spoke to the people:
> *I am the light of the world;*
> *anyone who follows me will not be walking in the dark;*
> *he will have the light of life.* (John 8:12)

During the "Sermon on the Mount" Jesus teaches:
> *You are the light of the world. A city built on a hill-top cannot be hidden. No one lights a lamp to put it under a tub; they put it on the lamp-stand where it shines for everyone in the house. In the same way your light must shine in the sight of men and women, so that, seeing your good works, they may give the praise to your Father in heaven.* (Matthew 5:14-16)

When to tell this story
This story fits well with the great festivals of light: Christmas and especially Easter when we renew our baptismal vows with lighted candles. It could also be used when teaching about the sacraments of baptism and confirmation.

Introduction
Talk about darkness and light. Get the children thinking about the great lights in the sky: the sun, the moon and the stars. Remind them that when the books of the Bible were written there were no electric lights.

Freddie and the power cut

It was a cold winter's evening. Freddie had had a good day at school and came home really pleased with a new book about animals found in different parts of the world. Some of them he knew about, but some he had never heard of before. Each child had been given a copy of the book and their task was to learn about three new animals.

The next day, the children would choose their favourite new animal and tell the rest of the class about it. Freddie was really interested and was going to look for an animal that he thought no one else would choose. After tea he went off to his room and started looking at all the beautiful photographs in the book. He had only just begun when, without warning, all the lights went out and his house was plunged into darkness. Freddie got up and began to take little steps very carefully towards the door, using his hands to feel where everything was. He banged his leg into the door and yelled out to his mum. A light was coming up the stairs, and there was his mum holding a torch. "There's been a power cut, Freddie," said his mum. "Will you come and help me find the pack of tealights which we can put safely around the house? We can light the candles we keep on the mantelpiece in the sitting room, as well."

"You've got that pretty flowery candle in the kitchen that Aunty Maggie gave you," remembered Freddie. "We can light up the house ready for dad and Suzie when they come home."

Freddie thought this was great fun and followed his mum around the house as she fished out tealights and placed them on saucers of water. As each little candle was lit, it shone out in the darkness and became a bright light for Freddie and his mum to walk around the house in safety.

"Freddie, we must be careful that they are not near anything which might catch fire," said his mum.

Gradually the house was transformed. The flickering lights made the house seem very pretty. Now in Freddie's sitting room there was a fireplace with a chimney which could be laid with logs or coal. When it was cold in the winter, Mum or Dad would light the fire for extra warmth. On this night Mum made up the fire and lit it, then placed the fireguard in front to make it safe. Soon the room began to warm up as well as brighten up, and it all seemed wonderfully cosy. A few minutes later Suzie came home from school with her dad. "You cannot see anything out there," Dad said, "but it's wonderful in here, so bright and cosy."

"You know, Freddie, this is the way people used to live before gas and electricity were discovered, and that's not so long ago. Just think, in the time of Jesus there were no electric lights, that's why we use candles in church, you know. It was because the friends of Jesus had to use candles to say Mass. It reminded them of Jesus saying, 'I am the light of the world.' Now you can see what Jesus meant, he lit up everybody's life and showed them the way to live happily and lovingly. Remember, Freddie and Suzie, he also said to us, 'You are the light of the world.'" Then, with a twinkle in his eye, Freddie's dad said: "So to you two bright sparks I say: keep your light burning brightly with smiles on your faces and a cheerful word for everyone."

Freddie's mum cooked a wonderful tea using a camping stove, and after tea they all sat around and his dad carried on teaching Freddie and Suzie about candles. "Do you remember on Easter Sunday that instead of saying the Creed, 'We believe in one God…', Father Anthony gave us all a candle and the servers lit them with the light they had taken from the Easter candle and we answered all the questions by saying loud and clear 'I do'? Those were the promises made at baptism. We made them for you when you were little babies so it's great you can make them for yourselves now. When you are confirmed you will make them again and be standing up and saying, 'I really am going to be your light in the world, Jesus.'"

It was just time for bed and guess what? Yes, the lights came back on again.

When Freddie went into school next day, Mrs Baxter asked all the children about their favourite animals. When she got to Freddie, he said: "I'm sorry, Mrs Baxter, but we had a power cut and I was never able to decide, but shall I tell you what happened?"

"You tell us," said Mrs Baxter, and Freddie ended up teaching the whole class about Jesus, the light of the world, and about baptism and confirmation.

Freddie and the school choir

Freddie and the school choir

The lesson
God has blessed us with lots of gifts. Some of us are good at number work, some good at writing, some good at singing, some good at sports and so on. This makes life really interesting, because together we can do so much to make life good and happy for ourselves and everybody else.

Scripture reference
Jesus told this parable about the kingdom of God:
> *It is like a man on his way abroad who summoned his servants and entrusted his property to them. To one he gave five talents, to another two, to a third one; each in proportion to his ability... The master came back and went through his accounts... The man who had received five talents came forward bringing five more... His master said to him, 'Well done, good and faithful servant.'* (Matthew 25:14-21)

When to tell this story
When you wish to help the children realise that we are all good at some things, but that not everybody can be good at everything. To help them not to be selfish over their gifts, for together we make the world go round.

Introduction
Have a chat with the children about what they think they are good at... better still, help them to identify the gifts they have noticed in one another.

Freddie and the school choir

Freddie's school was becoming famous for the children's singing. The music teacher, Mr Bandoretti, was great fun and all the children loved him. He believed that everybody can sing and make music and that all we need is a bit of encouragement. Some children were learning to play musical instruments and others were able to experiment with percussion instruments during the singing lessons.

School assemblies every Friday were times when everyone was encouraged to sing their very best. The Head Teacher used to remind the children that when they were singing they were praying twice over. He used to say, "The angels in heaven have a fantastic band and choir and spend lots of their time praising God and thanking God for all his love and goodness. When we sing, let us imagine ourselves joining the angels in heaven in their songs of praise."

The singing became so good that one day the local television company sent a camera crew to record the children and they appeared on the local news that evening. Freddie and his school were becoming quite famous!

It was not long after, that Mr Bandoretti announced to the whole school that the school choir had been invited to take part in "The National Competition for Primary School Choirs", to be televised on the national network.

This was becoming really exciting. They had to learn special songs for the competition and the great day came when they would have to go to London and be judged in the Royal Albert Hall.

It was the day of the competition; there were people everywhere. The children from the other schools were buzzing with excitement and very friendly. They cheered and clapped all the performances. The standard of singing was amazingly high.

When Freddie's school was called, they went behind the stage to prepare. Mr Bandoretti could see they were a little nervous but he smiled and calmed them down as he said, "Now children, you know how much you love singing. Just imagine you are back at a school assembly and think of the angels singing along with you; but most of all, think of all the people in the hall and the people at home, who will watch you on television, and remember your job is to use this wonderful gift God has given you to make them all happy."

When the judges gave their verdict at the end of the day, they said that there were so many wonderful performances that it was almost impossible to choose between the schools, but only one school sang with such obvious joy in their hearts that they had to be the winners. Yes, it was Freddie's school! Mr Bandoretti's little speech had done the trick.

Then something even more amazing happened. Just before they got back on the bus, Mr Bandoretti said to Freddie: "Come with me;

someone wants to interview you." Freddie realised he had been chosen to speak on behalf of the school. The television interviewer was very nice and first asked Freddie his name.

"Freddie Freckles," he said.

"Now Freddie," she said, "everyone watching you, the judges, the camera crew and all the other children, teachers and parents noticed that you all enjoy singing so much that you have smiles on your faces all the time."

"Oh yes," said Freddie, "that's because we have the angels singing with us, and we sing because God has given us our voices so that we can sing his praises and make everyone happy. In fact Mr Bandoretti is always reminding us that singing is only one of the many gifts God has given us. We all have different gifts and the important thing is that we use our gifts to make this a happier and better world."

"Well Freddie, that's a terrific message and I want you to know that what you have said is absolutely true. Already we have had lots of calls from viewers, saying how happy you have made them. In fact one old lady said she jumped out of her chair and danced around the room: something she hasn't done for a long, long time.

"Congratulations to you all on your wonderful performance. It gives me great pleasure to present you with this cup on behalf of your school."

Freddie shows courage

Freddie shows courage

The lesson
Bullying can be a real problem, even among young children. This story is designed to remind children to stand up to bullies in the right way.

Scripture reference
Matthew 10:16-20 has Jesus reminding his apostles that when they are in trouble they are not to worry: *what you are to say will be given to you when the time comes.*

When to tell this story
It would be appropriate to tell this story if you have concerns that the children are having problems among themselves. You might also consider it appropriate when a new group is forming, for example, at the beginning of a school year, as a new class settles in.

Introduction
Talk to the children about some of the difficulties that we encounter when we have a group of friends and someone else arrives on the scene. Also, if appropriate, raise the question of bullying.

Freddie shows courage

Freddie was very lucky. He had a really good group of friends, which included Peter Pickles, Tom Goodman and Clare Wilson. Although they were special friends, and we all need special friends, they liked to try to get on with everyone else. But there was one boy in the class who was very difficult to get on with and generally they stayed out of his way; his name was Rodney. Rodney was big and strong and very bossy. He had a little gang, some of whom were older than Rodney and who used to meet on the playground and chase the other boys and girls.

One day a few weeks after the term had started a new boy arrived in the school. His name was Michael. It was difficult to get to know Michael because he was so shy. He didn't want to join in their games, but just sat in a corner of the playground, reading a book or playing his own private games. Freddie began to feel sorry for Michael and became very concerned when he noticed that Rodney was beginning to pick on Michael. It was only in little ways, but they were enough for him to realise that these things were making Michael very unhappy.

One evening at home, Freddie was sitting very quietly, thinking about all this, and his dad noticed how thoughtful he was.

"Freddie, are you all right?" asked his dad.

"I'm fine thanks, Dad," Freddie said, but his dad knew he wasn't. His dad wondered whether maybe Freddie was being bullied, but at the time he didn't ask Freddie any more questions. Later in the evening his dad found the right moment to tell Freddie about a boy who used to bully him at school, and how he had stood up to the bully and solved the problem. He knew that the story might give Freddie something to think about and might help him if he was facing a problem.

Next day at school, Freddie was thinking to himself, "I must stand up to Rodney and stop him bullying Michael." It was not long before he got his chance. The bell had rung for the end of playtime and everyone was lining up ready to go back into class. As they began to file into the classroom in silence, Freddie noticed that Rodney quietly tried to trip up Michael as they went up the steps. In a big loud voice, Freddie shouted at Rodney, "Don't you ever do that again!" Freddie was trembling with fear and anger because he knew that Rodney was bigger than he was and might take it out on him later, but he was determined that he had to be strong and make a stand. Immediately one of the teachers came over and asked what was going on.

Now Freddie didn't hesitate. "I have to tell you, Mrs Thomas, that Rodney has been bullying Michael and I just noticed him trying to trip Michael up as we went back to class." Mrs Thomas, who was a teacher of the older children, called Rodney and Michael to come to her and then took the three of them up to the classroom and spoke to their own teacher. Mrs Baxter took Mrs Thomas to one side and spoke quietly, so that the children were not sure what was going to happen. Then she sent them to their places and said she would see them at the end of the morning. This gave them all time to think.

At lunchtime Mrs Baxter began the conversation by asking Michael how he was settling into the school, and he admitted that it was not easy and that he was missing his old friends. "Why are you being unkind to Michael?" she asked Rodney, and he looked down ashamed, unable to answer. "This has to stop immediately and I will be watching to make sure that you all behave in a proper way towards one another," she said. "And you, Freddie, well done! We need more children willing to stand up for what is right and to look after one another."

From that day Michael was able to relax and became real friends with Freddie's group; and although it took Rodney a few days, he gradually became a much more friendly person and he certainly stopped his bullying.

At the end of the week Freddie's dad noticed how cheerful he had become, singing away to himself and getting on with everything with a cheerful smile on his face. "Had a good week, have you, Freddie?" he asked.

Freddie told him the story and his dad smiled quietly to himself.

Freddie and his new fishing rod

Freddie and his new fishing rod

The lesson
Obedience is important. Our parents and teachers know what is best for us and how to keep us safe. It is weakness, not strength, to be tempted to give in to others who may be pressurising us.

Scripture reference
Children, be obedient to your parents in the Lord – that is your duty. (Ephesians 6:1)

When to tell this story
The story is a basic one concerned with obedience and with not being led astray. It could be told whenever you consider it appropriate.

Introduction
Have a discussion about how easily we can be led astray and how we hate to be accused of being cowardly.

Freddie and his new fishing rod

It was Saturday morning and Freddie had set off for the shops to buy himself a few sweets for the weekend. He was looking in the sports shop when his Uncle George came by and tapped him on the shoulder. "Hello, Freddie," he said, "what are you looking at?"

"Oh, Uncle George," he said, "I am looking at that super fishing rod, which is being offered at a bargain price. I will never be able to save up for that."

"Would you really like it, Freddie?" said his uncle.

"I would just love it, uncle," said Freddie.

"Then it is yours," said his uncle. He was always spoiling Freddie, and Freddie's mum was always pleading with her brother not to.

They went into the shop and the assistant came over. "I am very fortunate," said Uncle George. "I have some spare money at the moment and I want to treat my nephew, Freddie, to that fishing rod you have in your window." The assistant carefully wrapped it up and gave it to Freddie. As they left the shop he hugged his uncle and thanked him and thanked him. He ran all the way home and rushed into the house shouting, "Guess what, guess what, guess what!"

"Calm down, Freddie," said his mum, "what is this all about?"

"Look," said Freddie. "Look at what Uncle George has just bought me."

His mum sighed and said, "I don't believe he has been spoiling you again. But listen, Freddie, that is a wonderful present and you may have it, but you must never go down to the river unless Dad is with you. Do you understand?"

"Yes, Mum, I promise," said Freddie

He knew that that morning his dad was due to be working on the bathroom and so he would have to wait before they could go fishing properly, but he asked if he could go to the park and his mum said he could. So off he went to look for Peter, who just happened to be coming down the road to find him. When Freddie showed him the fishing rod, he could hardly believe it and said, "Freddie, that's great, let's go off to the river to catch some fish."

"Oh no," said Freddie, "I can only go to the park; my mum said so."

"She'll never know," said Peter. "Come on, let's go to the river."

"No," said Freddie, "it's not right."

"You are a big baby," said Peter.

"I'm not," said Freddie, and so they went on arguing for some minutes until Freddie stamped his foot and said, "I'm not a big baby, I'm not, I'm not, I'm not. All right, let's go to the river."

Freddie felt very bad inside, but they went down to the river and prepared the rod the best they could. Freddie really needed his dad to show him, but he put some bread onto the hook and tried to cast the line into the river. He had seen bigger boys and girls doing it so easily, but after a few tries the line still only just reached the edge of the water. Peter teased him, telling him he would never catch any fish there. He suggested he climb up the tree overhanging the water and simply drop the line straight down into the river. Again they had an argument, Freddie saying that it was dangerous and Peter telling him he was a big baby. Again it ended with Freddie screaming that he was not a baby and climbing up the tree with the rod on his back. Eventually he managed to drop the line into the water, as he clung nervously to the branch.

He was just about to climb down again when suddenly he felt the line tighten and he realised he must have a fish on the hook.

"Oh," he cried, "I think I've caught a fish." He tried desperately to reel in the fish, but the big fish was not going to be caught that easily. It battled with Freddie, who was struggling to keep steady, and then as the branch began to sway the fish gave a big tug and Freddie fell straight into the water.

Now even Peter Pickles was getting worried. He jumped up and down shouting, "Help, help, help, my friend is in the river."

They were very lucky. A fisherman a little further upstream was packing up to go home and heard all the commotion. Leaving the bank, he jumped on his bike and pedalled swiftly along the towpath. He could see Freddie frantically fighting to stay afloat because, although he could swim, the current was very strong. The fisherman waded in and brought Freddie back to the bank and safety. He asked what had happened and Freddie began to tell the tale. Through his sobs he was stuttering and stammering that his uncle had bought him the fishing rod and that he was only supposed to go to the park but that Peter had called him "a big baby" and they had come to the river after all.

John, the fisherman, reckoned that it would be helpful to accompany the boys back home. He didn't want the young lad to be put off fishing after only one attempt at a sport which he had enjoyed ever since he was a boy.

You can imagine what a reception Freddie received from his mum. Peter tried to explain that it was all his fault, but Mrs Freckles reminded him that Freddie had a mind and a will of his own and he would have to learn to be obedient.

Freddie learnt an important lesson that day. He was not allowed out on his own for two weeks and then his dad took him to the river to learn how to fish properly. Actually he also learnt quite a bit from his new fishing friend John, as well.

But from that day onwards Freddie never let anyone change his mind just because they called him names.

Freddie and the football match

Freddie and the football match

The lesson
When we cheat or misbehave in any way, we must learn to say sorry. Asking forgiveness, and forgiving people who hurt or upset us, is central to the teaching of Jesus.

Scripture references
Jesus tells us that there must be no limit to the times we are willing to forgive:
> *Peter went up to Jesus and said, "Lord, how often must I forgive my brother if he wrongs me? As often as seven times?" Jesus answered, "Not seven, I tell you, but seventy-seven times."* (Matthew 18:21-22)

Jesus prayed for those who had crucified him:
> *Father, forgive them; they do not know what they are doing.* (Luke 23:34)

Then there is the parable of the Prodigal Son (Luke 15:11-32); Jesus giving his apostles the authority to forgive sins on Easter night (John 20:20-23) and Jesus' many encounters with sinners in the Gospels.

When to tell this story
This story may be used when preparing children for the sacrament of reconciliation and indeed when talking about contrition and forgiveness in general.

Introduction
Discuss with the children how they feel when they know they have done wrong and also how they feel when they have the courage to own up and are forgiven. Talk about what it feels like when someone says "sorry" to you.

Freddie and the football match

It was Saturday morning and a bright autumn day – just perfect for football in the park. Freddie, Peter, Tom and quite a few of the boys from their class were up for it and Peter's dad was free to organise a six-a-side match.

There was a corner of the park they liked to play in because it was an ideal size for such a match and as usual they piled their tracksuit tops together to make the goalposts. Freddie was a good goalkeeper, though he also liked to play in other positions as well. That morning he agreed to play in goal and they had a terrific match. He played superbly, tipping the ball round the posts on a number of occasions and catching everything that came his way. They had been playing for some time and Peter's dad said they would play for just five more minutes before they had a break.

The score was 2-1 to Freddie's team and everyone played really hard for those last few minutes; Freddie's team trying to hang on to their lead and Peter's team trying to get an equaliser.

Then suddenly Tom got the ball and beat three players before closing in on Freddie's goal. He struck a brilliant shot, which even Freddie couldn't reach, and the ball sailed just inside the goal. As Freddie turned he saw the ball flying through the air and he knew it was inside the tracksuit-top goalposts, but he jumped up and screamed that the ball had hit the post. Some of the other boys protested, but Peter's dad wasn't sure and said that if Freddie said so, he would take his word for it, and the goal was not given.

As they were going back for a break, Tom and Peter went over to Freddie and called him "a cheat", and Freddie got very angry and shouted back at them. Mr Pickles came over and calmed everyone down, but he could see that they were all still very cross and were not speaking to one another as they ate the biscuits and gulped down the squash that Mrs Pickles had ready for them.

Deep down, Freddie began to feel very bad. He knew he had cheated. He had wanted to win so much that he tried to convince himself that maybe the ball had just struck what *would have been* the post. But his conscience (that voice deep down inside him) was telling him otherwise. He stood up and said, "I'm sorry, you were right, it *was* a goal. I was wrong to pretend that it had hit the post."

Mr Pickles came over and told Freddie he had been brave to admit he was wrong, and he called on all the other boys to forgive him. Then he announced that due to Freddie's honesty, in the end the match had been drawn 2-2.

Both teams finished the contest cheering each other for a good morning's game. It was a special moment for Freddie and his friends.

In fact they became even better friends because of what had happened and Freddie had learnt a really important lesson that day. When you are big enough and brave enough to admit that you are wrong and allow yourself to be forgiven, it is then that you grow stronger as a person.

Freddie and the birthday party

Freddie and the birthday party

The lesson
This is a story to help the children understand that the Mass can be understood as having a meal with Jesus.

Scripture references
Mark 14:12-16. 22-25: Mark tells the story of the Last Supper.

Acts 2:42-47: In Acts we are told how the early Christians met in one another's homes for the Mass.

John 6:1-15: The feeding of the five thousand: John includes in the story the little boy who was generous enough to share.

When to tell this story
Whenever you wish to teach the children about the Mass.
It is also a story that would be suitable in preparation for First Holy Communion.

Introduction
Talk with the children about parties. What are the occasions when we have parties? If we are guests, what do we usually take with us? How do we dress? What sort of things do we do at parties? Talk a lot about the food we eat.

Parallels to look for: gifts given and received; food and drink; united in love as one big family; even the singing of songs to express our joy.

Freddie and the birthday party

It was Peter Pickles' birthday and Freddie couldn't wait until Saturday, the day of the party. They would have a great time with all their friends. He saved up some pocket money and went into town to buy Peter a present, which he knew he would like. Peter had a great collection of toy cars and Freddie had noticed a new one in the shop, which he knew Peter didn't have in his collection.

When Saturday came, Freddie was up early and could think only of the party. He wrapped up the present and wrote his card, telling Peter how pleased he was that they were such good friends and wishing him every happiness not just for his birthday but for the whole of the next year.

He arrived at Peter's house at the same time as lots of others. Apart from Peter's school friends, Mr and Mrs Pickles had also invited some of the children who were living in a special home for refugees. Refugees are children and adults who have had to leave their own countries because it is dangerous for their families to live there any more. Mrs Pickles had got to know them as she was helping them to learn English. All Peter's friends knew that they were special guests and enjoyed looking after them. Smiles and welcoming looks communicated just as well as words, though it was interesting hearing another language being spoken.

It was a beautiful sunny afternoon and Peter's dad had arranged some brilliant games in the garden. Everyone joined in and had a great time. When they came into the house for the birthday tea their eyes lit up. It was simply fantastic. There was everything that everyone could possibly want and in the middle of the table was a huge birthday cake with eight candles.

They munched their way through sandwiches and crisps, pizza and sausages, jelly and chocolate marshmallows and all sorts of delicious food. When the time came for the cake, they all sang "Happy Birthday" to Peter and he blew out the candles in just one long breath.

Mrs Pickles cut up the cake and wrapped up a piece for each child, and put it into a party bag which they could take home.

It was just the way Jesus wanted his gatherings to be: everyone looking after one another and everyone having enough to eat.

In fact at the end of the tea Mr Pickles told the children that this was just the time to say a "thank-you" prayer together and they all joined hands and prayed quietly. As many of them were in the First Communion class he reminded them that going to Mass was like going to Jesus' party. "We don't take Jesus toy cars," he said, smiling and winking at Freddie, "but we can take him our hearts and our lives. He doesn't give us pizza and sausages, but the greatest food possible: himself, in Holy

Communion; food to make us strong and loving inside. So let us thank Jesus today for the good time we have had and let us ask him to bless all our special guests whose smiling faces tell us they have enjoyed our party. "Let us also pray that we may always come to his party, the Mass, with smiling faces and kindness in our hearts, ready to receive Holy Communion with reverence and love. Amen."

The children all said "Amen" and then they thanked Mr and Mrs Pickles and Peter and got ready to go home, taking with them the happiness of the day and ready to share it with their own families.

That too is something Jesus wants us to do after we have been to *his* party: to take his love out into the world and share it with everyone else.